What My Little Boy Is Made Of

A MEMORY BOOK

paintings by
Jim Daly

H HARVEST HOUSE PUBLISHERS

EUGENE, OREGON

WHAT MY LITTLE BOY IS MADE OF

Text copyright © 2005 by Harvest House Publishers
Eugene, Oregon 97402

ISBN 0-7369-1446-3

Artwork copyright © Jim Daly and may not be reproduced without
permission. For more information regarding art prints featured in this
book, please contact:

    Jim Daly
    P.O. Box 25146
    Eugene, OR 97402
    Email: caroledaly@comcast.net

Design and production by Koechel Peterson & Associates, Inc.,
Minneapolis, Minnesota

Printed in China

05 06 07 08 09 10 11 12 13 /IM/ 10 9 8 7 6 5 4 3 2

*Often God's biggest gifts to us come in
the littlest of packages...our children.*

❖❖❖

ANONYMOUS

Great Expectations

The day I discovered you were coming into my life, I _____

_____

_____

_____

I prepared for your arrival by _____

_____

_____

_____

My hopes for my future son were _____

_____

_____

_____

My first prayer for you was _____

_____

_____

_____

A child's life has no dates, it is free, silent, dateless.
A child's life ought to be a child's life, full of simplicity.

❖❖❖

OSWALD CHAMBERS

Boys are found everywhere on top of, underneath, inside of, climbing on, swinging from, running around or jumping to. Mothers love them, little girls hate them, older sisters and brothers tolerate them, adults ignore them and Heaven protects them.

❖ ❖ ❖

ALAN BECK

The Day You Arrived

When I saw your sweet face, I _____

_____

_____

_____

Everyone who met you would say _____

_____

_____

_____

Your name was chosen just for you because _____

_____

_____

_____

I knew you were a special boy when _____

_____

_____

_____

The Gift of You

Your presence in my life taught me to _____

_____

_____

_____

Having a little boy changed my life because _____

_____

_____

_____

Every time I held you, my heart overflowed with thoughts of

_____

_____

_____

I thanked God for many things about you, but most of all for

_____

_____

_____

*A fairly bright boy is far more intelligent and
far better company than the average adult.*

❖ ❖ ❖

JOHN B. S. HALDANE

*Each child is an adventure into a better life—an opportunity
to change the old pattern and make it new.*

❖❖❖

HUBERT H. HUMPHREY

Action and Adventure

Your favorite game of make-believe was _____

_____

_____

Often you wanted to dress like the superhero or character of

_____

_____

With your imagination you could turn a cardboard box or a

front porch into _____

_____

_____

Your ideal adventure was _____

_____

_____

Whenever I wasn't looking, you tried to get into _____

_____

_____

A Day in the Life of You

Your morning ritual was _____

_____

_____

At mealtimes we used to _____

_____

_____

Your favorite part of the day was _____

_____

_____

Bath time was always an adventure because you _____

_____

_____

Our evening routine to lull you to sleep was _____

_____

_____

There was never a child so lovely but his mother
was glad to get him to sleep.

❖❖❖

RALPH WALDO EMERSON

*Nothing could stay or turn him aside, while his mother's words
lingered in his ear. No harm could fall on a head made sacred by
her blessing, and no evil enter a heart filled with such holy love.*

❖ ❖ ❖

LOUISA MAY ALCOTT

Oh, the Things You Say

Humorous, sweet, and clever things you have said.

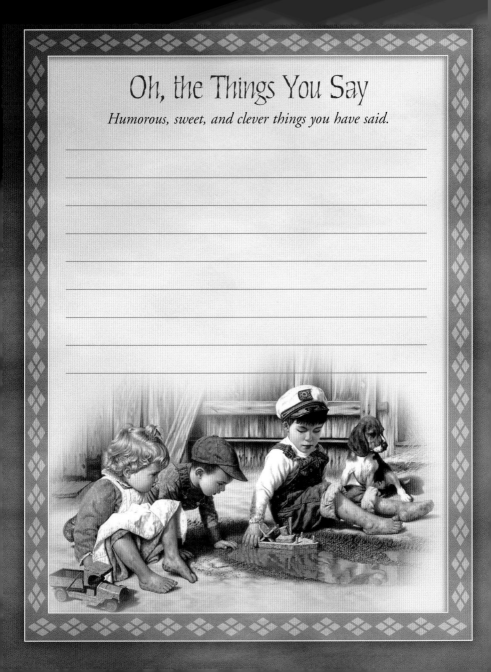

*For unflagging interest and enjoyment, a household of children,
if things go reasonably well, certainly makes all other forms of
success and achievement lose their importance by comparison.*

❖ ❖ ❖

THEODORE ROOSEVELT

Steps of the Journey

I always smile when I think of the time you _____

_____

_____

_____

I cry when I remember _____

_____

_____

_____

One of your biggest trials/obstacles as a child was _____

_____

_____

_____

Pride filled my heart many times, especially when _____

_____

_____

_____

Heart and Soul

You found comfort in _____

_____

_____

_____

When you talked to God, you _____

_____

_____

_____

The gifts of the heart you shared with others were _____

_____

_____

_____

You showed courage when _____

_____

_____

_____

Scenes from Your Life

Memorable moments through the ages.

When you were a newborn (cuddling, crying, awakening):_____

_____

_____

When you were 1 to 3 (walking, talking, connecting with others):

_____

_____

When you were 4 to 6 (making friends, going to school, playing):

_____

_____

*I remember seeing a picture of an old man addressing a small boy.
"How old are you?" the old man asks. "Well, if you go by what
Mama says," the boy responds, "I'm five. But if you go by the
fun I've had, I'm almost a hundred."*

❖ ❖ ❖

WILLIAM LYONS PHELPS

It was the policy of the good old gentleman to make his children feel that home was the happiest place in the world; and I value this delicious home-feeling as one of the choicest gifts a parent can bestow.

❖❖❖

<small>WASHINGTON IRVING</small>

Legacy and Love of Family

The people who make your family include _____

_____

_____

The family traditions you loved most were _____

_____

_____

Our family pets were _____

_____

You enjoyed family outings such as _____

_____

_____

I can see the legacy of others in your face and personality.

You seem so much like _____

_____

_____

A Few of Your Favorite Things

Favorite books/toys: _____

_____

Things that made you laugh: _____

_____

Your ideal backyard would have _____

_____

Favorite animals: _____

_____

When I was in a hurry, your favorite stall tactic was _____

_____

_____

_____

Favorite music: _____

_____

_____

A perfect day for you would include _____

_____

Favorite sports and games: _____

_____

You said you absolutely had to have a _____

_____

Favorite subject to learn about: _____

_____

Favorite thing to do with your daddy: _____

_____

Never be surprised when you shake a cherry tree if a boy drops out of it;
never be disturbed when you think yourself in complete solitude
if you discover a boy peering out at you from a fence corner.

❖❖❖

DAVID GRAYSON

Laughter and Joy

Your favorite game to play in the car was _____

_____

_____

Your favorite friends over the years were _____

_____

_____

You could entertain yourself for hours by _____

_____

_____

Songs you liked to sing: _____

_____

_____

When playing with other kids, you _____

_____

_____

_____

Only You

I have never met a child who had your _____

_____

_____

_____

You expressed creativity by _____

_____

_____

_____

You strived for your independence most by _____

_____

_____

_____

Even as a young child, you were able to _____

_____

_____

_____

*Each child is created in the special image and likeness of God
for greater things—to love and be loved.*

❖❖❖

MOTHER TERESA

We worry about what a child will become tomorrow,
yet we forget that he is someone today.

❖ ❖ ❖

STACIA TAUSCHER

Dreams of Becoming

I thought you might grow up to be a _____

because you always _____

_____

_____

_____

You said you wanted to be a _____ some day.

I caught a glimpse of the man you would become when ____

_____

_____

_____

My prayers for your future are _____

_____

_____

_____

_____

Growing Up So Fast

The day I realized you were no longer a baby but a little boy was

_____

_____

_____

_____

To act older you _____

_____

_____

_____

_____

As you grow older, the most important thing to remember is

_____

_____

_____

_____

_____

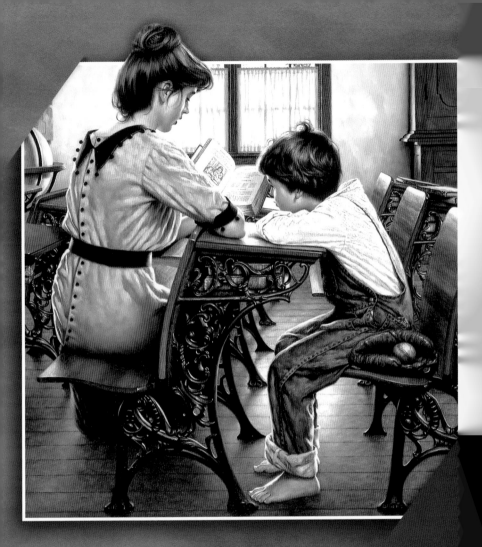

Don't let anyone think little of you because you are young.
Be their ideal...be a pattern for them in your love,
your faith, and your clean thoughts.

❖ ❖ ❖

THE BOOK OF FIRST TIMOTHY

What Life Is Made Of: My Letter to You

*When one asked him what boys
should learn, "That," said he,
"which they shall use when men."*

❖ ❖ ❖

PLUTARCH

Dear _____,

From the day you came into my life, we were off and running. Our days were filled with exciting escapades (real and imagined), personal discoveries, and stories of far-off lands.

You have taught me to treasure the adventure of life. Now I offer you a treasure chest of memories from these early years. May they remind us both of the laughter, courage, and wonder that shaped your path toward becoming a man.

Love,

_____